BY **ANGUS McGILL & DOMINIC POELSMA**

CLIVE is featured daily in the London *Evening Standard*

Published by
W. H. ALLEN
London
1970

I THINK I'M THE VICTIM OF CRADLE SWAPPING! SOMEONE SAW ME IN MY BEAUTIFUL ROYAL CRADLE AND SWAPPED ME FOR AN ORDINARY LITTLE GIRL IN HER ROTTEN ORDINARY CRADLE!

WHERE ARE YOU TAKING ENID TONIGHT CLIVE ?

OH I DON'T KNOW...

WE MAY GO TO THE PICTURES OR WE MAY GO DANCING OR WE MAY JUST MOOCH AROUND...

IT DEPENDS HOW MUCH MONEY SHE'S GOT.
Roelsma
189

ENID'S VERY LATE! WHERE ON EARTH CAN SHE BE ?

OH SHE CAME ABOUT HALF AN HOUR AGO. BUT CRIPPEN WOULD N'T LET HER IN.

CRIPPEN HATES BLONDES
BEWARE OF THE CAT
Roelsma
190

I'VE NEVER BEEN SO HUMILIATED! I CALL FOR YOU AND YOUR BEASTLY CAT DOESN'T LET ME IN!

WHY SHOULD I ALWAYS HAVE TO CALL FOR YOU ANYWAY? BOYS USUALLY CALL ON GIRLS!

OH NOW BE REASONABLE, ENID!

Poelsma
YOU KNOW IT TAKES ME FAR LONGER TO GET READY.
191

I'VE GOT A SECRET!
WHAT IS IT? WHAT IS IT? TELL ME QUICK! I LOVE SECRETS!

MY BROTHER CLIVE IS GOING TO MARRY PRINCESS ANNE!

194

PRINCESS ANNE WHO?
Poelsma

ISN'T THAT JOHN LENNON?

IT IS! IT IS JOHN LENNON!

NO, IT'S JUST HARRY BUTTON TRYING TO LOOK LIKE JOHN LENNON.
HARRY **BUTTON**!
Poelsma

WHO DOES HE THINK HE'S KIDDING?
195

I'M **SURE** THAT'S JOHN LENNON.

I MUST SPEAK TO HIM. I **MUST**!

EXCUSE ME. BUT YOU **ARE** JOHN LENNON?
NO I'M HARRY BUTTON
196

IMPOSTOR!
Poelsma

AS IF ANYONE WOULD BELIEVE THAT WAS REALLY JOHN LENNON!

IT'S SO OBVIOUSLY HARRY BUTTON PRETENDING TO BE JOHN LENNON!

UNLESS OF COURSE IT'S JOHN LENNON PRETENDING TO BE HARRY BUTTON PRETENDING TO BE JOHN LENNON!
Roelsma

JOHN!
197

I WAS LORD KITCHENE
VALET'S AUNTIE

I WAS LORD KITCHENER'S VALET'S AUNTIE
Roelsma

AAARGH!
206

KEEP OUT GO AWAY!
BUT MOTHER IT'S ONLY ME!
CLIVE? ARE YOU SURE?
OF COURSE I'M SURE.
Poelsma
SLAM!
AAAARGH!
207

TAKE OFF THAT STUPID FAKE MOUSTACHE AND THOSE RIDICULOUS SPECS THIS MINUTE!
AND WHY PRAY?

BECAUSE THEY MAKE YOU LOOK LUDICROUS AND BECAUSE THEY FRIGHTEN YOUR MOTHER AND BECAUSE I SAY SO!

I THINK THEY LOOK BEEZER!

Poelsma
208
IF AUGUSTA THINKS THEY LOOK BEEZER, BEEZER IS HOW THEY LOOK!

OW!

OOOUCH!

THERE SHOULD BE A WARNING ON THE PACKET!
Roelsma 209

HEY ENID! ENID! ENID BABY! WELL IF IT ISN'T THE LOVELY ENID! WHAT'S YOUR HURRY ENID? EEEENID!

THAT WAS ENID.
Roelsma
214

I THOUGHT I'D GIVE A PARTY...

JUST A FEW FRIENDS, A FEW LAUGHS, SOME MUSIC PERHAPS ...

Poelsma
ARE WE INSURED?
215

AUGUSTA, I'M GIVING A PARTY NEXT WEEK AND ...
A PARTY! BEEZER! I LOVE PARTIES!

ICE-CREAM AND CREAM CAKES AND TRIFLE AND JELLY AND MORE ICE-CREAM AND LOTS AND LOTS OF LEMONADE...
AND YOU WILL HAVE TO GO TO BED AND STAY THERE!

IT'S GOING TO BE A GROWN-UP PARTY. YOU CAN'T COME!
AND MUSICAL CHAIRS AND POSTMAN'S KNOCK AND CHARADES AND SARDINES AND MURDER!

AUGUSTA!
AND I'LL WEAR MY NEW PINK DRESS WITH MY NEW PINK SHOES AND I'LL GET A PINK RIBBON FOR MY HAIR AND...
Poelsma
216

I'M HAVING A PARTY ON SATURDAY. COME ALONG.

I'M HAVING A PARTY ON SATURDAY. WHY DON'T YOU CATS LOOK IN?

PARTY. SATURDAY. MY PLACE.

I SUSPECT I HAVE A FLAIR FOR THIS SORT OF THING!
217

HEY ENID! ARE YOU COMING TO MY PARTY?

IT DEPENDS. I MIGHT HAVE SOMETHING NICER TO DO. I MEAN THERE MIGHT BE SOMETHING ON TELEVISION OR I MIGHT WANT TO WASH MY HAIR. OR I MIGHT WANT TO SIT AND THINK ABOUT THINGS.

OR SOMEONE MIGHT ASK ME TO ANOTHER PARTY. IT MIGHT BE JOHN LENNON. I MIGHT PICK UP THE PHONE AND HE MIGHT SAY "THIS IS JOHN LENNON. COME TO MY PARTY!"

SO IT DEPENDS...
218

NOW LOOK HERE. MY PARTY'S ON SATURDAY. YOU ARE GOING OUT AREN'T YOU!

BUT AREN'T WE INVITED?
INVITED? OF COURSE YOU'RE NOT INVITED!

Poelsma
219
WHERE DID WE GO WRONG?

AS APPARENTLY YOU THINK US TOO OLD TO COME TO YOUR PARTY. WE ARE GOING OUT TO ENJOY OURSELVES.

WE WILL TAKE IN A SHOW, DINE BY CANDLE LIGHT AND DANCE UNTIL DAWN!

Poelsma
WE'LL BE BACK ABOUT HALF PAST ELEVEN!
220

THIS IS GOING TO BE ONE OF THE GREAT PARTIES!

AUGUSTA'S SAFELY IN BED. MY PARENTS ARE SAFELY OUT.

IT WILL BE THE WILDEST, CRAZIEST, MOST FANTASTIC PARTY THIS TOWN HAS EVER...

HOW DO I LOOK?
KISS ME
221
Poelsma

KISS ME

SOME PARTY!
KISS ME
Poelsma
222

HELP!
Roelsma

RING RING
KNOCK KNOCK
RING RING

I DO HAVE RATHER A FLAIR FOR THIS SORT OF THING...
223

KISS ME
WELL! WHAT ABOUT SOME PARTY GAMES?

WHO'S FOR ANIMAL, VEGETABLE, MINERAL? WHO'S FOR CONSEQUENCES?

WHAT ABOUT CHARADES? LET'S HAVE SOME CHARADES! COME ON! WHAT'S WRONG WITH CHARADES!
Roelsma
224
SOME PARTY!

WHAT ON EARTH ARE YOU DOING, AUGUSTA?

AUGUSTA!

RIGHT! WE'RE READY! LET'S START!

NOT MUSICAL CHAIRS!
225

HEY COME NEXT DOOR. THEY'VE GOT THIS REAL KICKY SCENE GOING. YOU'LL BLOW YOUR MIND!

226
ISS
E
BLIND MAN'S BUFF!

AUGUSTA RUINED MY PARTY!

ALL THE GROOVIEST KIDS IN TOWN AND SHE HAD THEM PLAYING STUPID PARTY GAMES! CONSEQUENCES! CHARADES! HUNT THE THIMBLE!

I'LL NEVER BE ABLE TO RAISE MY HEAD IN THE HIPPY-A-GO-GO AGAIN!
IT WAS BEEZER!
Roeloms
227

EXCUSE ME.

Roeloms
228

HEY SANDY! HELLO SANDY!

HELLO ENID! WHO'S THE FELLER?
OH HIM? IT'S ONLY CLIVE.
OH. WELL GOOD-NIGHT.
GOODNIGHT.

229

I'VE MADE A LIST OF ALL THE CHRISTMAS PRESENTS I HAVE TO BUY AND I'VE COUNTED ALL THE MONEY IN MY PIGGY BANK AND THE SITUATION IS NOT GOOD...

CHRISTMAS PRESENTS; 15s 11d CASH IN HAND; 4d DEBIT BALANCE 15s7d I MUST MAKE ECONOMIES.

I KNOW! WE'LL TAKE **YOU** OFF THE LIST.

THAT SAVES 8d
246

IF ONLY YOU'D LISTEN TO MY ADVICE, I WOULDN'T **NEED** 14s11d FOR CHRISTMAS PRESENTS!

AND WHAT PRAY, IS YOUR BRILLIANT ADVICE?

OH, IT'S SO SIMPLE...

Poelsma
MARRY PRINCESS ANNE!
247

JUST SUPPOSING..

JUST SUPPOSING CLIVE MARRIED PRINCESS ANNE..

JUST SUPPOSING CLIVE MARRIED PRINCESS ANNE AND WE WENT FOR TEA TO BUCKINGHAM PALACE...
Poelsma

DO YOU SUPPOSE THE QUEEN WOULD LEND ME 14s11d?
248

WHAT ARE YOU GIVING ME FOR CHRISTMAS CLIVE?
NO — LET ME GUESS. A RING. THAT'S RIGHT ISN'T IT? A LOVELY RING.

A PLATINUM RING WITH AN ENORMOUS DIAMOND, SET ABOUT WITH EMERALDS AND RUBIES, WITH A LITTLE CARD THAT SAYS 'TO ENID, BECAUSE SHE IS SO LOVELY!'

THANK YOU CLIVE.

ROLL ON CHRISTMAS.
249
Poelsma

I SENT THREE CHRISTMAS CARDS!

AND I GOT SEVEN.

SO I WIN!
Poelsma
254

I'M DEFORMED!

HOW CAN I EVER EVEN LEAVE THE HOUSE?

MY LIFE IS RUINED!

MY SIDEBOARDS WON'T GROW!
Poelsma
258

CLIVEY CAN'T GROW SIDE-BOARDS, CLIVEY CAN'T GROW SIDEBOARDS!
SHUT UP!

IT'S TRUE, IT'S TRUE, YOU CAN'T GROW SIDEBOARDS!
WELL? CAN YOU?

I'M DEFORMED!
Poelsma
259

DARLING, HAVE YOU SEEN MY FUR COAT?

IT'S GONE! IT'S BEEN STOLEN. WE'VE BEEN BURGLED! MY BEAUTIFUL...

NEW...
Poelsma

FUR COAT!
261

YOU HAVEN'T BEEN OUT IN YOUR MOTHER'S MUSQUASH!

WEREN'T YOU ASHAMED TO BE SEEN?

WELL, YES I WAS REALLY.
Poelsma

YOU SEE I MET ROBSON. HE WAS IN HIS MOTHER'S MINK!
262

Poelsma

AHEM!

HI!

FOR GOODNESS SAKE! DON'T YOU RECOGNISE ME?

IT'S ME. ENID!

WELL WHY DIDN'T YOU SAY SO IN THE FIRST PLACE?
296

MY MOTHER'S COMING FOR THE WEEKEND.

OH NO! SO IS MINE!

NO!
NOT BOTH TOGETHER!

WHEN IT COMES TO GRANDMAS, ONE'S COMPANY, TWO'S WAR...
Poelsma
297

YOUR GRANDMOTHER WILL BE HERE ANY MOMENT. SHE'LL BE RATHER TIRED SO DON'T MAKE A NOISE AND.. OH HELP— THERE'S THE BELL..
DARLING!
HELLO MOTHER!

THIS **CAN'T** BE LITTLE CLIVE! HOW BIG AND STRONG YOU'VE GROWN! AUGUSTA SEEMS MUCH THE SAME!

COOCHIE FACE! DARLING! LET'S HAVE A DRINKIE.
LIZ!

WHATEVER HAPPENED TO GRANDMAS?
298

GRANDMA, DID YOU KNOW THAT OUR OTHER GRANDMA IS COMING AS WELL.
NO!

YES MOTHER, MRS. BRAVO WILL BE HERE ANY MINUTE, SO PLEASE **BEHAVE!**
I'LL GO! I WON'T STAY IN THE SAME HOUSE AS THAT WOMAN I'LL...
RING! RRRING!

HELLO DEAR.
HELLO MOTHER.

HELLO MRS. QUINCY! YOU LOOK AWFUL, DEAR. WHY DON'T YOU HAVE A NICE LIE DOWN? WE'RE NONE OF US GETTING ANY YOUNGER..

SEE WHAT I MEAN!
299

GERRRRRRRRA

MOTHER!
GRANDMA!
WHAT IS IT? WHAT'S HAPPENING?
YOU'VE WOKEN CRIPPEN!
OWOUUUUUU

PUBLIC OPINION MEANS NOTHING TO GRANDMAS.
OWOOOOOUUUUUO
Poelsma
300

HELLO GRANDMA!
PLEASE! NEVER CALL ME THAT AGAIN!

IT'S BAD ENOUGH BEING ONE! THERE'S NO NEED TO REMIND ME ALL THE TIME. CALL ME LIZ.
OH! ALL RIGHT!

WHAT ABOUT YOU, GRANDMA? SHOULD WE CALL YOU HANNAH?

Poelsma

GRANDMAS CAN BE VERY CONFUSING!
301

WE HAVE TO CALL GRANDMA BRAVO "GRANDMA" AND GRANDMA QUINCY "LIZ"...

OH DEAR!

THIS IS TERRIBLE!

302
I CAN NEVER REMEMBER WHICH IS WHICH!
Poelsma

COME AND PEEL THE POTATOES CHILD, MANY HANDS MAKE LIGHT WORK...

ALL RIGHT GRANDMA BRAVO. ARE YOU GOING TO HELP TOO GRANDMA LIZ?

NO DARLING. TOO MANY COOKS SPOIL THE CONSOMMÉ.

YOU CAN LEARN A LOT FROM GRANDMAS.
Poelsma
303

THERE ! YOU'RE FINISHED. NOW IT'S CLIVE'S TURN.

CLIVE! YOUR BATH'S READY!
CLIVE! GRANDMA'S WAITING!

CLIVE? HAS ANYONE SEEN CLIVE ?
CLIVEY ! CLIVEY!

306

OH COME, MOTHER. DON'T YOU THINK CLIVE IS OLD ENOUGH TO BATH HIMSELF?

FIDDLESTICKS! THE LAD'S AFRAID OF A LITTLE SOAP AND WATER. JUST LIKE YOU!

COME ON NOW! UPSTAIRS WITH YOU. MUSN'T WASTE THAT GOOD HOT WATER!

EDWIN! EDWIN ! HAS ANYONE SEEN EDWIN?
307

IS IT TRUE THAT YOU'VE HAD FOUR HUSBANDS GRANDMA ?
YES DARLING.

AND OUR OTHER GRANDMA HAS ONLY HAD ONE ?
THAT'S TRUE DARLING.

WELL I THINK IT'S JOLLY UNFAIR.

COULDN'T YOU HAVE LOANED HER ONE OF YOURS ?
308

WHEN I GROW UP I'M GOING TO HAVE FOUR HUSBANDS..

AND WE'LL ALL LIVE TOGETHER IN A PRETTY LITTLE HOUSE AND...
YOU CAN'T DO THAT. YOU CAN ONLY HAVE ONE HUSBAND AT A TIME!

ONLY ONE AT A TIME?

HUH!

THAT'S ALL **YOU** KNOW...
309

MOTHER I'M VERY WORRIED ABOUT EDWIN!

HE'S DRINKING TOO MUCH! HE'S GAMBLING! HE'S ALWAYS SHORT OF MONEY

HE'S **ALWAYS** WORKING LATE AT THE OFFICE. HE NEVER TAKES ME OUT. I'M SURE THERE'S ANOTHER WOMAN! HE'S LOSING HIS HAIR...
LOSING HIS HAIR!

OH MY POOR BABY!
310

GRANDMA...
YES DARLING?

WHAT WAS IT LIKE IN THE OLDEN DAYS?

I NEED A VERY LARGE DRINK...
311

WHEN I WAS A LITTLE GIRL THERE WAS NO SUCH THING AS TELEVISION.

THERE WERE NO MOTOR CARS OR AEROPLANES OR TELEPHONES OR CINEMAS OR WASHING-MACHINES OR ELECTRIC LIGHT OR REFRIGERATORS OR ELECTRIC COOKERS ...

WHAT ABOUT ELECTRIC TOOTHBRUSHES? DIDN'T YOU HAVE ELECTRIC TOOTHBRUSHES? NO? YOU DIDN'T HAVE ELECTRIC TOOTHBRUSHES?

FANTASTIC! AMAZING! WAIT TILL I TELL CLIVE THIS! NO ELECTRIC TOOTH-BRUSHES! WOW!
HOW ON EARTH DID WE MANAGE?
Roelsma
312

GOODBYE DARLINGS. IT'S BEEN SUCH FUN!

OR RATHER IT'S BEEN QUITE FUN...

OR PERHAPS I SHOULD SAY IT'S BEEN FUN SOME OF THE TIME...

OR TO BE MORE ACCURATE THERE HAVE BEEN MOMENTS WHEN...
Roelsma
313

BODY BUILDING MADE EASY

RIGHT. NOW PUNCH ME IN THE STOMACH. GO ON. PUNCH ME IN THE...

BODY BUILDING IS **FUN**!
314

ALL RIGHT. YOU CAN OPEN YOUR EYES AGAIN...

TOM AND JERRY'S OVER NOW...
315

DON'T TELL ME YOUR PARENTS STILL WAIT UP FOR YOU!

RIDICULOUS! AT YOUR AGE! YOU SHOULD HAVE GOT THEM TRAINED BY NOW!

323
Roelsma

ODEON
I SOMETIMES WONDER WHETHER WE'RE COMPATIBLE.

TICKETS
TWO BACKSTALLS PLEASE...

WE'RE COMPATIBLE!
344
Roelsma

I NEARLY WROTE A BEAUTIFUL POEM ABOUT YOU LAST NIGHT.
Roelsma

REALLY?
YES. IT COULD VERY WELL HAVE MADE YOU IMMORTAL.

WHAT STOPPED YOU THEN?

I COULDN'T THINK OF A SINGLE RHYME FOR 'ENID'.
345

MOTHER I'M WORRIED ABOUT CLIVE!

SUPPOSING HE FAILS HIS 'A' LEVELS...

SUPPOSING HE FAILS HIS 'A' LEVELS AND CAN'T GET INTO COLLEGE AND CAN'T GET A JOB AND HANGS AROUND LOW CLUBS ALL DAY AND TAKES TO DRINK AND BECOMES A HOPELESS DRUNKARD AND ABSOLUTELY RUINS HIS LIFE...
Roelsma

I'M WORRIED ABOUT CLIVE!
358

MOTHER IT'S ABOUT CLIVE! I'M SO WORRIED!

SUPPOSING HE'S **SEDUCED** BY THAT AWFUL ENID!

SUPPOSING HE GETS HER INTO TROUBLE · OR SHE **SAYS** HE'S GOT HER INTO TROUBLE. AND HE HAS TO MARRY HER AND SHE LEADS HIM A DOG'S LIFE AND RUNS ABOUT WITH OTHER MEN AND LEAVES HIM AND THE LITTLE ONES TO FEND FOR THEMSELVES ...

359
WILL IT BE OUR FAULT?

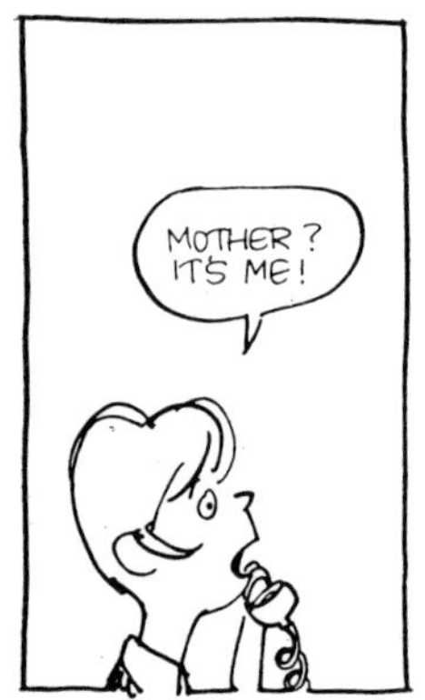
MOTHER? IT'S ME!

I'VE BEEN AWAKE ALL NIGHT WORRYING ABOUT CLIVE!

SUPPOSING HE GETS INTO BAD COMPANY! SUPPOSING HE GETS INTO BAD COMPANY AND STARTS TAKING DRUGS AND BECOMES AN ADDICT AND GETS ARRESTED AND IS THROWN INTO JAIL AND IS **FORCED** INTO A **LIFE OF CRIME**!

360
WHERE DID WE GO WRONG?

YOU NEVER EVER PAY ME A COMPLIMENT.

VICTOR

Roelsma

YOU FASCINATING LITTLE WITCH!
367

CLIVE. IT'S ENID!

SHE'S WEARING A NEW ORANGE DRESS WITH WHITE DOTS AND A FRILL ROUND THE BOTTOM...
Roelsma

BUT SHE'S GOT THE SAME OLD HAIR DO AND THE SAME OLD SHOES AND THE SAME OLD HANDBAG AND THE SAME OLD BEADS SHE GOT FOR CHRISTMAS!

HE'LL BE RIGHT DOWN....
375

THE GIRLS AT THE OFFICE WERE ASKING ME WHAT YOU WERE LIKE TODAY.

I SAID YOU WERE **FABULOUS**!

I HOPE WE DON'T MEET ANY OF THE GIRLS FROM THE OFFICE!
376

CLIVE... DO YOU REMEMBER OUR VERY FIRST DATE?

DO I!

DO I?

NO I DON'T
377

WE'RE NOT COMPATIBLE!
378

IT'S A LOVELY DAY SO WE'RE GOING TO THE SEASIDE.

HOORAY! HOORAY! HOORAY! HOORAY! HOORAY!

THE SEASIDE? THAT IS WHERE THE SEA IS, ISN'T IT?
YES.

427
HOORAY! HOORAY! HOORAY! HOORAY! HOORAY!
Roelsma

WE'RE GOING TO THE SEASIDE!

WE'RE GOING TO THE SEASIDE TO FEED THE WHALES!
NO DEAR. THERE AREN'T ANY WHALES AT THE SEASIDE!
Poelsma

NO WHALES! NO WHALES AT THE SEASIDE! HEE HEE HEE HEE HEE HEE...

428
I HOPE WHALES LIKE SARDINE AND PEANUT BUTTER SANDWICHES.

IS THIS THE SEASIDE?
YES DEAR THIS IS THE SEASIDE.

HOORAY! HOORAY! HOORAY! HOORAY!
Poelsma

429
WHICH IS THE SEA?

DO YOU MIND!

430
Poelsma

NOW LOOK WHAT YOU'VE DONE! YOU'VE WET MY LOVELY NEW BATHING COSTUME!

431
STUPID SEA!
Poelsma

Poelsma

432

Poelsma

433
RUDE!

CLIVE, WHY DOES THE SEA GO IN AND OUT LIKE THAT?
Poelsma

BECAUSE OF THE MOON.
THE MOON?

TEE HEE HEE HEE HEE HEE!

434
MUMMY, WHY DOES THE SEA GO IN AND OUT LIKE THAT?

KISS ME QUICK
Poelsma

KISS ME QUICK

KISS ME QUICK

435
CAN I CHANGE IT? THIS ONE SEEMS BROKEN!

KISS ME QUICK

KISS ME QUICK

KISS ME QUICK

Poelsma 436
ISS QUICK

WHERE'S LITTLE AUGUSTA ?

SHE'S BEACH-COMBING.

SO FAR SHE'S FOUND 14 SHELLS, 35 PEBBLES, TWO TRANSISTOR RADIOS, A PICNIC BASKET, THREE BEACH BALLS, 17 BEACH TOWELS, TWO DECK CHAIRS, A JELLY FISH ...

437
LOOK WHAT I FOUND, LOOK WHAT I FOUND!
AND CHARLES ATLAS JUNIOR!
Poelsma

DO YOU KNOW WHAT MR. ROBINSON HAD THE NERVE TO SAY TO ME TODAY?
Poelsma

HE SAID I WAS UNPUNCTUAL, CARELESS AND INEFFICIENT, THAT MY TYPING WAS A DISGRACE AND MY SPELLING NOT TO BE BELIEVED!

BUT MR. ROBINSON I SAID, I'M THE ENGLISH ROSE TYPE!

445
THAT PUT HIM IN HIS PLACE!

MY MOTHER HAS BEEN WARNING ME AGAINST MILLIONAIRES.

DO YOU KNOW WHAT THEY DO? THEY LEAD YOUNG GIRLS ASTRAY BY TAKING THEM TO EXPENSIVE RESTAURANTS AND GLAMOROUS NIGHT CLUBS!

THEY TEMPT THEM WITH BEAUTIFUL CLOTHES AND COSTLY FURS. THEY FLATTER THEM AND PURSUE THEM AND LOAD THEM DOWN WITH COSTLY JEWELS!
Poelsma

446
HOW DO YOU MEET MILLIONAIRES?

I'M TOLD THAT SOMETIMES MILLIONAIRES DRESS IN ORDINARY CLOTHES AND MINGLE WITH THE PEOPLE.

THEY'RE LOOKING FOR YOUNG GIRLS TO LEAD ASTRAY!

Roelsma

447
IF ANY OF THEM ARE, HERE, THEY CAN'T BE LOOKING VERY HARD!

WHY DON'T YOU INTRODUCE ME TO SOME MILLIONAIRES?

ARE YOU ASHAMED OF ME OR SOMETHING? DO YOU THINK I WOULDN'T KNOW HOW TO BEHAVE IN THE PRESENCE OF MILLIONAIRES?

I KNOW EXACTLY HOW TO BEHAVE. YOU FLING YOURSELF IN THEIR ARMS AND COVER THEM IN KISSES. THAT'S WHAT MILLIONAIRES LIKE.
Roelsma

448
SO WHY DON'T YOU INTRODUCE ME TO SOME MILLIONAIRES?

EXCUSE ME, SIR, ARE YOU A MILLIONAIRE?
NO! I'M NOT A MILLIONAIRE.

449
THEN TAKE YOUR HANDS OFF MY KNEE!

CLIVE, DO YOU THINK MILLIONAIRES ARE ATTRACTED TO THE ENGLISH ROSE TYPE?

BEING THE ENGLISH ROSE TYPE MYSELF, THIS IS SOMETHING THAT NATURALLY INTERESTS ME.

WHAT DO YOU THINK? DO YOU THINK MILLIONAIRES ARE ATTRACTED TO THE ENGLISH ROSE TYPE?
WELL ER, THAT IS TO SAY...

450
JUST AS I THOUGHT **EVERYONE** IS ATTRACTED TO THE ENGLISH ROSE TYPE...

PETAL... WHERE ARE ALL MY WOOLLY VESTS ?

AND WHERE'S MY DEFENCE MEDAL ? AND WHERE'S MY OLD DAD'S WATCH CHAIN ?
I KEEP LOSING THINGS TOO. I'VE LOST MY NEW FELT HAT AND MY NICE CHAIN BELT AND MY CHIFFON SCARF AND...
Poelsma

456

I THINK CLIVE'S READING ONE OF THOSE AWFUL RUDE BOOKS !
WHAT !

HE WAS SO BUSY READING IT HE DIDN'T HEAR ME COME INTO HIS ROOM THEN HE WENT BRIGHT RED AND HID IT UNDER THE BED CLOTHES !
WE'LL SEE ABOUT THAT !

YOUNG MAN GIVE ME THAT BOOK !

462
"JUST WILLIAM !"
Poelsma

YOUR DADDY AND I ARE GOING OUT TONIGHT. HE'S TAKING ME TO THE THEATRE! AND CLIVE WILL BE OUT TOO, SO...

YOU'RE ALL GOING OUT! LEAVING LITTLE ME ALL ALONE WITH THE BOGY MEN?

DON'T BE SILLY DEAR. THERE AREN'T ANY BOGY MEN. AND ANYWAY BERYL NEXT DOOR WILL BE BABY SITTING...
BERYL NEXT DOOR!
Roelsma

I THINK ON THE WHOLE, I'D RATHER HAVE THE BOGY MEN.
463

AH, BERYL. COME TO BABY SIT FOR US EH?

THAT'S RIGHT MR. BRAVO. AND THIS IS MY FRIEND BERT. HE'S GOING TO KEEP ME COMPANY!
OH, BUT BERYL...

Roelsma
WELL, I COULDN'T STAY IN THE HOUSE BY MYSELF COULD I?

WHAT ABOUT THE BOGY MEN?
464

GOODNIGHT AUGUSTA. IF YOU WANT ANYTHING BERYL NEXT DOOR IS BABY SITTING DOWNSTAIRS
HA!

AND SHE'S BROUGHT HER YOUNG MAN WITH HER TO KEEP HER COMPANY!
HA!
Roelsma

NOW DON'T WORRY DARLING. LITTLE AUGUSTA WILL BE ALL RIGHT. BERYL IS A NICE, SENSIBLE GIRL AND...

HA!
465

HA!

YOU CALL THAT BABY SITTING?
Roelsma

466

I THINK THAT AWFUL BERYL NEXT DOOR IS AFTER CLIVE!
CLIVE!

AND I'D BEEN THINKING SHE WAS AFTER ME!
475

OH LOOK! THERE'S BERYL NEXT DOOR. I THINK SHE'S GOING TO SUNBATHE!

CLIVE! LOOK! SHE'S WAVING HER HANKY AT YOU!

NOW SHE'S WAVING HER BEACH-HAT!

NOW SHE'S WAVING THE TOP OF HER...

476
RUDE!

FOR ME ? THANK YOU BERYL !
Poelsma

SO MUCH FOR SAYING IT WITH FLOWERS !
477

I THINK BERYL NEXT DOOR REALLY FANCIES YOU CLIVE.
WHAT EVER MAKES YOU THINK THAT ?

OH I DON'T KNOW...

I LOVE YOU CLIVE
I LOVE CLIVE BRAVO
I LOVE YOU CLIVE
BERYL LOVES CLIVE
WOMAN'S INTUITION I SUPPOSE.
478
Poelsma

I DO EVERYTHING I CAN TO MAKE YOUR BROTHER NOTICE ME! BUT I DON'T THINK HE EVEN KNOWS WHO I AM!
Roelsma

DON'T WORRY! IT'S ALL RIGHT!

HE DOES KNOW WHO YOU ARE! HE SAYS YOU'RE BERYL NEXT DOOR!
479

WHAT'S ALL THIS I HEAR ABOUT BERYL NEXT DOOR?
Roelsma

EVERYONE SAYS SHE'S IN LOVE WITH YOU!
IN LOVE WITH **ME**?

OF COURSE I DON'T TAKE ANY NOTICE!

I MEAN, HOW COULD **ANY** GIRL BE IN LOVE WITH **YOU**?
480

HEY! GRANDMA QUINCY IS JUST COMING UP THE PATH!
WHAT!

QUICK! AUGUSTA PUT YOUR TOYS AWAY! CLIVE CLEAR THE TABLE! EDWIN TIDY UP A BIT!
GRRRRR

CLIVE! DRY THE DISHES! AUGUSTA, PUT YOUR NEW DRESS ON! EDWIN **DO SOMETHING!**
Roelsma

481
MOTHER! WHAT A LOVELY SURPRISE!

DARLINGS, THIS IS LUIGI. HE'S MY NEW CHAUFFEUR!

YOUR CHAUFFEUR, MOTHER? HAVE YOU BOUGHT A CAR?

DON'T BE ABSURD DARLING.

482
I COULDN'T AFFORD LUIGI **AND** A CAR!
Roelsma

LUIGI COMES FROM SUNNY SPAIN.
EETALY!

HIS FATHER IS A BARONE.
EES DUCA!

LUIGI IS A **VERY** OLD FRIEND.
WE MEET LAST TUESDAY!

HE IS **VERY** HANDSOME
AH...

483
EES RIGHT!

MOTHER! HOW COULD YOU BRING THAT AWFUL YOUNG MAN TO THE HOUSE!

LUIGI? BUT HE'S A DIVINE YOUNG MAN. SUCH BEAUTIFUL MANNERS. YOU HAVE MADE QUITE AN IMPRESSION. HE THINKS YOU ARE VERY BEAUTIFUL AND MYSTERIOUS!
BEAUTIFUL AND MYSTERIOUS?

BEAUTIFUL AND MYSTERIOUS!

BEAUTIFUL AND MYSTERIOUS!

484
LUIGI, WOULD YOU LIKE A CUP OF TEA?

EEEK!

MOTHER! YOUR AWFUL YOUNG MAN PINCHED MY BOTTOM!
Roelsma

THERE! WHAT DID I TELL YOU!

485
HE HAS **BEAUTIFUL** MANNERS!

Roelsma

AUGUSTA! DON'T STARE AT LUIGI. IT'S RUDE.
EES NOT RUDE. EES NATURAL! SHE STARE BECAUSE LUIGI EES SO HANDSOME!

THAT'S RIGHT MUMMY.

486
AND ALSO BECAUSE IF I STARE LONG ENOUGH, HE MIGHT GIVE ME SIXPENCE!

TELL ME! WHO EES THAT LADY, SO BEAUTIFUL AND MYSTERIOUS?

BEAUTIFUL AND MYSTERIOUS LADY! WHO ON EARTH DO YOU MEAN?
THE BEAUTIFUL AND MYSTERIOUS LADY WHO BRINGS ME ALL THESE CUPS OF TEA!

OH, HER! SHE'S NOT A BEAUTIFUL AND MYSTERIOUS LADY...

487
SHE'S JUST MY MUM!
Roelsma

OH GRANDMA...
DON'T CALL ME THAT!
Roelsma

ALL RIGHT GRANDMA
WHAT A DEPLORABLE CHILD YOU ARE!

BUT GRANDMA...
LUIGI, CALL A CAB. WE ARE LEAVING AT ONCE.

488
GOOD BYE GRANDMA!

MEN!

YOU'RE ALL THE SAME!
Roelsma

YOU'RE JUST AFTER ONE THING...

OUR MONEY!
TICKETS
489

STOP THAT!
Roelsma

BUT I WASN'T DOING ANYTHING!
YOU WEREN'T?

I'M TERRIBLY SORRY! I THOUGHT IT WAS MY FRIEND!
490

WHAT A **BEAUTIFUL** FILM!
ODEON
Poelsma

I LOVE A FILM WITH A HAPPY ENDING!
BUT IT DIDN'T HAVE A HAPPY ENDING.

SHE SHOT HIM DIDN'T SHE?

I CAN'T **IMAGINE** A HAPPIER ENDING!
491

I THINK MR. ROBINSON FANCIES ME!

I GOT IN FIRST FOR A CHANGE THIS MORNING. SO WHEN HE ARRIVED I GAVE HIM MY SMILE AND I SAID GOOD MORNING. "GOOD MORNING MR. ROBINSON." I SAID, JUST LIKE THAT!

HE GAVE ME ONE LOOK AND WALKED STRAIGHT INTO HIS OWN OFFICE AND CLOSED THE DOOR!

Poelsma
I THINK HE FANCIES ME!
496

I'VE WRITTEN A POEM. IT'S CALLED "TO ENID"
Roelsma

TO ENID "ROSES ARE RED..."
NOT NECESSARILY.

WHAT DO YOU MEAN. NOT NECESSARILY?
ROSES AREN'T NECESSARILY RED. THEY CAN BE WHITE OR CREAM OR YELLOW OR APRICOT OR ORANGE OR PINK OR A SORT OF ROSY SALMON OR A KIND OF LILAC MAUVE OR PALE MAGENTA. THEY CAN ALSO BE LIGHT VERMILLION.

I KNOW BECAUSE I AM MYSELF THE ENGLISH ROSE TYPE! BUT DO GO ON.

TO ENID. ROSES ARE WHITE OR CREAM OR YELLOW OR APRICOT OR ORANGE OR PINK OR A SORT OF ROSY SALMON OR...
498

!
AUGUSTA! GO UPSTAIRS THIS MINUTE AND WASH YOUR DIRTY FACE!

JUST TELL ME ONE THING! WOULD YOU TELL THE QUEEN TO GO UPSTAIRS THIS MINUTE AND WASH HER DIRTY FACE?
YES I WOULD!

OH NO!

SHE'LL CHOP YOUR HEAD OFF!
Roelsma
499

"SHALL I COMPARE THEE TO A SUMMER'S DAY?

CERTAINLY NOT!

WHO DO YOU THINK YOU ARE, ANYWAY? YOU KEEP YOUR NASTY COMPARISONS TO YOURSELF, SLOB FACE!
Poelsma

504

HELLO CLIVE. HERE'S A LETTER FOR YOU!
FOR ME! THANK YOU BERYL.

DEAR CLIVE, I LOVE YOU. I'M CRAZY ABOUT YOU. I ADORE YOU. YOURS FAITHFULLY, A. WELLWISHER.

A. WELLWISHER?

516
MUM. DO WE KNOW ANYONE CALLED WELLWISHER?
Poelsma

BERYL NEXT DOOR HAS JUST HANDED ME THIS ANONYMOUS LETTER.
Roelsma

I LOVE YOU. I'M CRAZY ABOUT YOU. I ADORE YOU. YOURS FAITHFULLY, A. WELLWISHER!

NO STAMP! NO POSTMARK!
AA! THAT PROVES IT!

IT'S FROM PRINCESS ANNE!
517

LOOK AUGUSTA! FOR ONCE AND FOR ALL I AM NOT MARRYING PRINCESS ANNE!

I KNOW WHAT IT IS. IT'S HER HATS!

CLIVE! DON'T WORRY ABOUT PRINCESS ANNE'S HATS!

518
IT'S JUST A PHASE...
Roelsma

TELL ME! WOULD YOU DESCRIBE ME AS BEING TANTALISINGLY LOVELY?
Roelsma

NO...

AS I SUSPECTED!

Roelsma
YOU NEED GLASSES!
527

CLIVE... I'VE BEEN THINKING!

IF ONLY WE WERE MARRIED, EVERYTHING WOULD BE PERFECT!

IF ONLY WE WERE MARRIED WE COULD START GOING TO WIFE-SWAPPING PARTIES AND I MIGHT END UP WITH SOMEONE SUPER!

SO WHY DON'T WE GET MARRIED?
Roelsma
534

YOU KNOW WHO YOU REMIND ME OF? THE EARLY BETTY GARBO!

BETTY GARBO? YOU MEAN **RITA** GARBO!
NO I DON'T! I MEAN BETTY GABLE

BETTY **GABLE**! THE NAME WAS **CLARK** GABLE!
OH VERY WELL!

540
YOU REMIND ME OF THE EARLY CLARK GABLE!
Poelsma

CLIVE! THAT MAN OVER THERE KEEPS STARING AT ME!

WHICH ONE?
THAT ONE!

THE ONE IN THE CAP?
NO THE ONE NEXT TO HIM WITH THE SIDE BOARDS! THE ONE THAT LOOKS A BIT LIKE ENGLEBERT HUMPERDINCK, ONLY FATTER!
Poelsma

547
THE ONE THAT'S SUDDENLY GONE VERY RED!

OH MY GOD!
Poelsma

THIS ISN'T HAPPENING!

HELP!

SHORT BACK AND SIDES PLEASE!
548

SHORT-BACK-AND-SIDES, DUCKIE? DO YOU MIND!
WELL...

NO-ONE GIVES SHORT-BACK-AND-SIDES IN THIS SALON DEAR! TRY WATERLOO STATION!
BUT...

PERHAPS WHAT YOU HAD IN YOUR TINY MIND WAS OUR NEW CHELSEA SHORTIE! SHORT AT THE BACK HERE, AND SHORT AT THE SIDES HERE!
THAT'S IT!
Poelsma

THEN WHY DIDN'T YOU SAY SO?
549

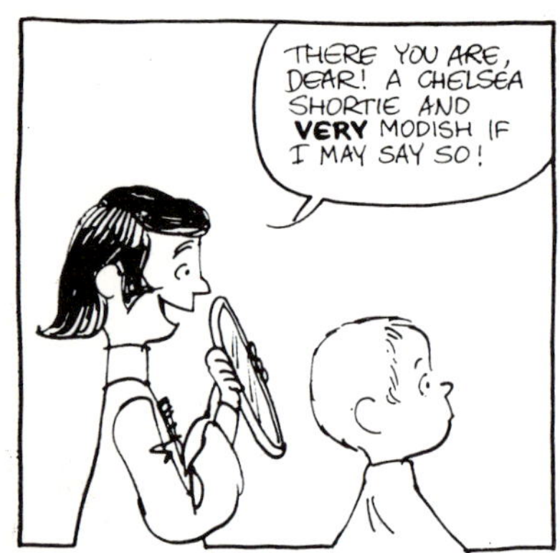
THERE YOU ARE, DEAR! A CHELSEA SHORTIE AND VERY MODISH IF I MAY SAY SO!

FACIAL TONE-UP? VIBRO-MASSAGE? VAPOUR RUB? MANICURE? PEDICURE? SAUNA IN THE BASEMENT? NO? DON'T STRAIN YOURSELF DUCKIE!

THAT WILL BE JUST TWENTY TWO AND SIXPENCE, LOVE! NOT FORGETTING SOMETHING FOR LITTLE ME...

550
WHAT HAVE I DONE?
Roelsma

CLIVE! YOUR HAIR! WHAT HAVE YOU DONE?

CLIVE! YOUR HAIR! WHAT HAVE YOU DONE?
GOOD HEAVENS WHAT HAVE YOU DONE?
Roelsma

FOR HEAVEN'S SAKE! I'VE HAD MY HAIR CUT! WHAT'S SO TERRIBLE ABOUT THAT!!

WHAT HAVE I DONE?
551

HAVEN'T YOU NOTICED ANYTHING?

LIKE WHAT!

LIKE YOUR HAIR BEING CUT YOU MEAN? IS THAT WHAT I'M SUPPOSED TO HAVE NOTICED? YOUR STUPID NEW HAIR CUT?
Roelsma

SHE NOTICED!
552

WANT TO START SOMETHING, SKINHEAD?

WHO D'YOU THINK YOU'RE KIDDING, FLASH?

WELL DONE, YOUNG MAN! NOT ALL THE YOUNG'UNS ARE GOIN' TO THE DOGS, EH?
Roelsma

553
PLEASE CAN I HAVE MY HAIR BACK?

DARLINGS!
Poelsma

GRANDMA YOU LOOK BEEZER!
THANK YOU DARLING!

AND LUIGI? EES HE NOT BEEZER ALSO?
OH YES, LUIGI YOU ARE VERY BEEZER!

EES TRUE!
561

CLIVE! YOU'VE HAD YOUR HAIR CUT! YOU LOOK PERFECTLY FRIGHTFUL!
AUGUSTA! WHAT A DRAB LITTLE DRESS!
Poelsma

PETAL! YOU REALLY MUST DO SOMETHING ABOUT YOURSELF! YOU ARE GETTING IMPOSSIBLY SUBURBAN!

562
WELCOME HOME GRANDMA!

GRANDMA, IN THE OLDEN DAYS, DID YOU HAVE COLOUR TELEVISION?

COLOUR TELEVISION? NOT THAT I RECALL!

BUT THEN, IN THOSE DAYS WE MADE OUR OWN ENTERTAINMENT! AS A MATTER OF FACT...
Roelsma

563
I STILL DO!

CLIVE! IT'S ENID!
Roelsma

SHE'S WEARING HER OLD DRESSING GOWN!
THIS IS **NOT** MY OLD DRESSING GOWN!

OH? SORRY!

575
CORRECTION SHE'S WEARING SOMEONE ELSE'S OLD DRESSING GOWN!

HELLO, ENID WAITING FOR CLIVE?
Poelsma

CLIVE, DEAR. ENID'S HERE!
IN AN OLD DRESSING GOWN!

AUGUSTA! THAT'S VERY RUDE. ENID ISN'T WEARING AN OLD DRESSING GOWN!

576
IT'S QUITE A NEW DRESSING GOWN!

HELLO ENID! HEY! THAT DRESSING GOWN LOOKS ALL RIGHT!

LOOK. LET'S GET THIS STRAIGHT THIS **ISN'T** A DRESSING GOWN!
Poelsma

NO?

577
THIS IS!

Poelsma

578
SEX MANIAC!

I THINK YOU LOOK LOVELY WITH YOUR HAIR SHORT, CLIVE.
Poelsma

I THOUGHT YOU LOOKED LOVELY WITH IT LONG AND NOW I THINK YOU LOOK LOVELY WITH IT SHORT.

WELL, THANK YOU BERYL!

I WILL CONVEY YOUR COMPLIMENTS TO CHIC STILE SALON (COIFFEURS FOR MEN) LTD.
579

CLIVE, WHY DON'T YOU GO AND BEAT SOMEONE UP?

BECAUSE THEY MIGHT BEAT ME UP BACK!

TRUE!

596
SO WHY DON'T YOU GO AND BEAT SOMEONE UP?
Poelsma

CLIVE! CLIVE!
Poelsma

QUICK GO AND KICK FREDDY BOSTON'S TEETH IN!

WHAT ON EARTH FOR?
OH, I DON'T KNOW.

597
IT'S SOMETHING TO DO!

Roelsma

598
PERSONALLY I BLAME TELEVISION.

HAVE YOU NOTICED THAT WHEN I SMILE THE MOST ENCHANTING LITTLE DIMPLE APPEARS?

THE MOST ENDEARING, LOVABLE, PROVOCATIVE LITTLE DIMPLE! HAVE YOU NOTICED?
NO I HAVEN'T!

606
THEN LOOK CLOSER!
Roelsma

607
Poelsma

HEY IT'S FREEZING LEND ME A BIT OF YOUR SCARF!

WOULD YOU LIKE SOME TOO?

608
Poelsma

CLIVE, DON'T YOU THINK I LOOK RATHER LIKE JOAN BAKEWELL ?
Poelsma

WELL — YES. YOU DO LOOK A LITTLE LIKE JOAN BAKEWELL...

609
EXCEPT FOR THE FACE...

I SUPPOSE YOU SENT ME THIS STUPID VALENTINE !

NO, I DIDN'T SEND ANYONE A VALENTINE.
YOU DIDN'T ? YOU'RE SURE YOU DIDN'T ?
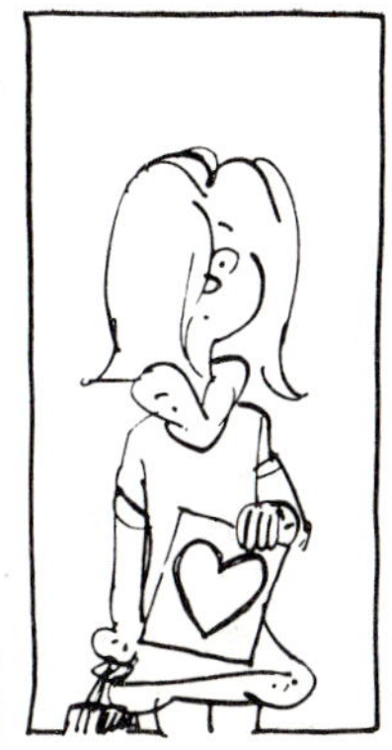

SOMEONE SENT ME A VALENTINE !
610

WHO COULD HAVE SENT ME THIS BEAUTIFUL VALENTINE?

PERHAPS IT WAS OUR MANAGING DIRECTOR. I KNOW HE'S MADLY IN LOVE WITH ME!

OR PERHAPS IT WAS ROBERT REDFORD! OR MICK JAGGER! OR PRINCE CHARLES!

THAT'S IT! **OF COURSE!** IT WAS PRINCE CHARLES!

WOMEN ARE NEVER WRONG ABOUT THESE THINGS!
Poelsma
611

CLIVE? ABOUT THIS VALENTINE!
OH NOT AGAIN!
Poelsma

WELL I'VE BEEN THINKING. PERHAPS IT WAS SENT TO ME BY A MYSTERIOUS STRANGER WHO HAS BEEN ADMIRING ME FROM AFAR!

A TRUE GENTLEMAN, TOO SHY TO MAKE HIMSELF KNOWN, TOO HONOURABLE TO FORCE HIS ATTENTIONS ON A PURE YOUNG GIRL!

SO IN THE SILENCE OF HIS LONELY ROOM, HE SENDS ME THIS TOKEN OF HIS LOVE...

KEEP AWAY FROM ME YOU DIRTY OLD MAN!
612

THAT MAN OVER THERE! HE'S STARING AT ME.
WHO? HIM? HE'S NOT STARING AT YOU!
Roelsma

HE'S NOT?
NO! HE'S NOT!

I FEEL ALL FUNNY... AAAAGH!
NOW IS HE STARING AT ME?
615

DO YOU KNOW WHAT DAY IT IS? IT'S OUR ANNIVERSARY!

JUST THINK! WE MET A YEAR AGO TODAY! SO WHERE ARE YOU TAKING ME?
Roelsma

ON A SENTIMENTAL JOURNEY!

VICTORIA
STATION CAFETERIA
622

DID ANYONE PINCH YOU TODAY ?

NO.
NOR ME !
Poelsma

UNDERGROUND
635
PERHAPS WE SHOULD TRY THE CENTRAL LINE !

WHO DID THAT ?
Poelsma

COME ON! WHO PINCHED MY BOTTOM ?

IT WAS I !

AND A GREAT BIG NON-EVENT IT TURNED OUT TO BE !
636

I KNOW WHAT YOU'RE THINKING!
Roelsma

VICTORIA
YOU'RE THINKING YOU'RE GOING TO DRINK CHAMPAGNE OUT OF MY SLIPPERS!

YOU'LL NOT ONLY RUIN MY SLIPPERS BUT THEY'LL BE ALL DAMP AND NASTY AND I'LL CATCH MY **DEATH** OF COLD!

646
SO FORGET IT!

CLIVE. WHY DON'T YOU PROPOSE TO ME?
PROPOSE TO YOU?

YES! PROPOSE! GO ON PROPOSE TO ME!
OH ALL RIGHT...

WILL YOU MARRY ME?
Roelsma

653
YOU MUST BE JOKING!

MUMMY! CLIVE'S KISSING ENID! HE IS. HE'S KISSING ENID!

HE'S KISSING HER HE'S KISSING HER!
Roelsma

654
RUDE!

Roelsma

BIG DEAL!
655

MUMMY!
WHAT IS IT NOW AUGUSTA?
Roelsma

ARE PEOPLE ALLOWED TO KISS PEOPLE?
WELL YES DEAR I THINK SO.

OH!

656
I THOUGHT THEY ONLY DID THAT ON TELEVISION!

MORNING AUGUSTA.
UUGH!

WHAT DO YOU MEAN UUGH?
I MEAN UUGH!

I MEAN KISSING ENID!
Roelsma

657
UUGH!

HELLO, GRANDMA
I'VE BROUGHT ENID TO SEE YOU

SO **THIS** IS LITTLE ENID!

DARLING, I'VE HEARD **SO** MUCH ABOUT YOU!
Poelsma

661
AND APPARENTLY EVERY **WORD** OF IT TRUE!

WELL, DARLING, SO YOU'VE KNOWN CLIVE FOR A WHOLE YEAR! SUCH A WASTE OF TIME!

AT YOUR AGE YOU SHOULD BE IDEALISTIC AND ROMANTIC YOU SHOULD BE THINKING OF IMPORTANT THINGS LIKE DIAMONDS AND ALLOWANCES AND THE CHANCES OF ALIMONY MY ADVICE DARLING IS CONCENTRATE ON OLDER MEN!
Poelsma

662
LEAVE THE YOUNGER MEN TO ME!

YOU'RE RIGHT MRS. QUINCY! I SHOULD GO AFTER OLDER MEN!

BUT THE ONLY OLDER MAN I KNOW IS MR. PRENDERGAST OF PERSONNEL AND HE'S GOT A WIFE AND SEVEN KIDS!

BUT IS HE RICH?
NO!

663
THEN FAREWELL MR. PRENDERGAST OF PERSONNEL!

I KNOW. LET'S PLAY CLIVE AND ENID.

I'LL BE CLIVE AND YOU BE ENID.
ALL RIGHT!

HELLO ENID, GET YOUR CLOTHES OFF!

685
TEE HEE
HEE HEE
HEE
HEE HEE
HEE
HEE
HEE
HEE
HEE HEE
HEE HEE

First published in Great Britain by W. H. Allen & Co. Ltd., 43 Essex Street, London WC2, and printed by Fletcher & Son Ltd., Norwich

ISBN 0 00046 4